Institute for Indigenous America Studies

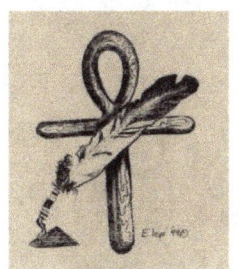

A short Story of the "Anisazi" Peoples of "America"
The history of America that vanished

Author: RaDine America-Harrison

Foundation for Indigenous America of

Anisazi Heritage

Quantum Leap SLC Publications

The information contained is not for public domain. Only private distribution from authorized personnel or subsidiaries. Publication is the sole property of the APH Private Trust; Cultural Library archives. All rights reserved.

ISBN # 0-9705455-6-8

A {short} Story of the Anisazi Peoples

Me Ma,

Whatever happened to the original/ indigenous race of PEOPLES, (females, males and children) their Earth soil, society, and culture living in America after Columbus found their part of the Earth?

Well child,

The story of my peoples is a long story….. But I am going to try to break it down for you to understand what became of us as a result of our section on Earth discovery by Columbus.

Now, when Columbus discovered the islands on the other side of the ocean from Europe, he discovered the Home with Earth for the brown-skinned, bushy-haired race of people who called themselves the Anisazi peoples , which translated as the "Ancient Ones" or the "Principled Ones", the keepers of the soil; the original People for the Earth.

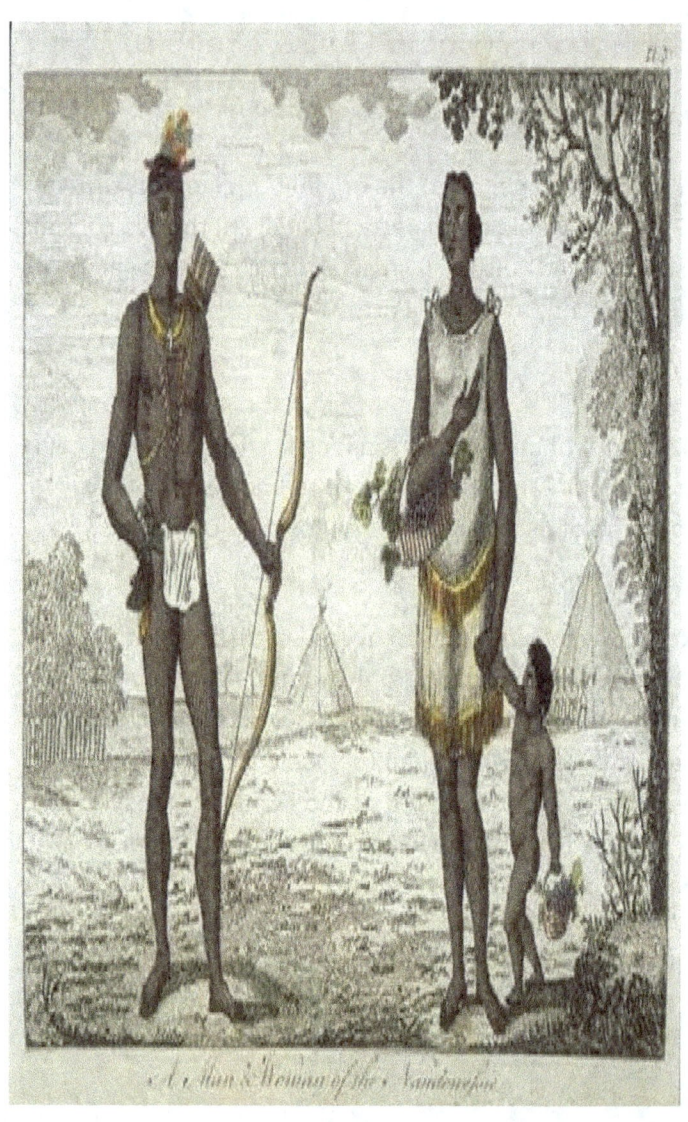

Painting of Amerindians of Georgia, USA, notice the hair is not straight or long and body build of the Anisazi female. (AHPT Research Dept.)

Columbus along with other European explorers named the new section of Earth and its well-developed societies and cultures living upon this newly discovered section of Earth - the "New World". Due to the tremendous size of this section for the planet Earth, estimated at being 10x bigger than Europe. The name given to this newly discovered section of the planet Earth, is the Western Hemisphere. The Anisazi people called their planetary home section with Earth "America". The European explorers adopted the Anisazi peoples name for their home with Earth and called the home with Earth for the Anisazi female race-the "Americas". They re-named the Anisazi race of people of the Americas - the American Indians or Amerindians.

All the Europeans foreigners exploring the Anisazi World in America, quickly discovered all the Anisazi people have basically the same physical characteristics for skin color. Regardless of how diverse the physique, the Anisazi race of people look like the soil of Earth to America. They are different shades of Earth soil from light to very dark skin, their hair reflects textures of the trees of the forest as different textures of wavy to bushy hair. To the dismay of the European foreigners , the Europeans quickly realized the indigenous dark skinned Anisazi peoples are a massive well-developed race consisting of hundreds of millions of people with a large portion of the population being females that covered every inch of the Earth's soil in the New World of the western hemisphere. European foreigners coined (nicknamed) the indigenous dark- skinned or brown , bushy- haired race , the "RED" race of people. The symbol used to represent the new World (called America) was a naked, tall, BROWN (dark) skinned, bushy- haired female. SEE BELOW

Picture below: Captured Anisazi females brought from North America to Europe in early 1700 and dressed in French attire. Look closely at the features.

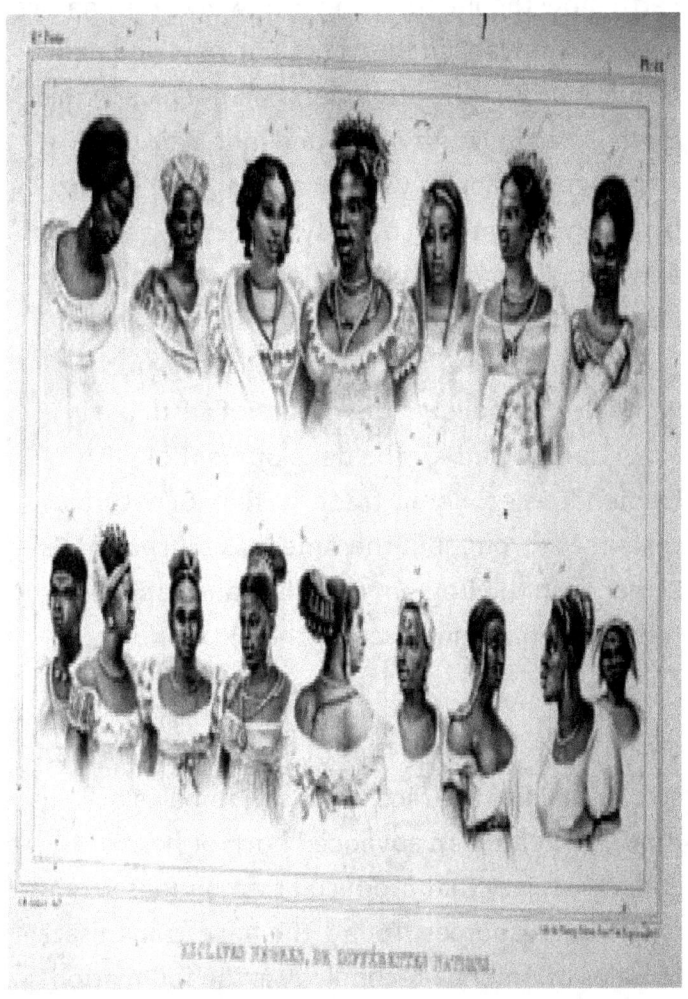

After 100 years of Roman/European foreigners freely exploring America, the Anisazi society and culture.

European foreigners discovered the Anisazi females of America's knowledge of the planet Earth ,how the life force of Earth works thru nature was more advanced than anything mankind had acquired from other conquests of peoples to the Earth living in North Africa and Indo Asia. The Anisazi technologies used to advance life in Earth by supporting the eco life system of trees, plants and animal life or forest to flourishes in America was very well developed .The Anisazi females of America use of her advanced technology for working with building the nature of Earth life in America, allowed for the development of a tremendous economic trade system of natural resources throughout the Americas that was, 10x bigger than the Roman feudalism and capitalistic trade systems being used by the old world in Europe.

The result from thousands of years under the stewardship of the race of Anisazi females of America created an advanced horti or perma cultural society that produced tremendous wealth of natural resources. Today, the ancestral Anisazi females of America technology is the foundation for **permaculture (maintain the ecosystem of the forest)** and Horticulture (growing plants for food) system we use today.

Horticulture is the foundation supporting the use for the application of agriculture.

The Anisazi people stated "their cultural civilization, was as old as the beginning of planetary Earth time for humans."

The Anisazi people technologic knowledge of the planet Earth allowed them to build huge pyramids structures created out of the soil of the Earth, called Mounds. Millions of these pyramids created from the soil of the Earth are all over America. The European foreigners to America named the ancient

Anisazi civilization in America the "Mound Builders".

The well-developed- Earth section as America represented the lost Garden of Eden to the European foreigners.

The European foreign explorers (men) desperately wanted to capture America the Garden of Eden as their trophy. Claiming America ,the Garden of Eden belonging to the Anisazi females of America as another expansion to their artificial homeland on Earth and subjugate to erase the future generations to be born from them.

The European foreigners on America's soil consciousness resolve is to conquest, the females of America, meaning to trick the people into a position allowing them to be controlled, pillaged, and exterminated. The new arrivals of females from Europe will replace the "life essence" to the race of Anisazi females of America belonging to the Garden of Eden, living in this enormously large sections of Earth, called the Western Hemisphere with the essence of their kind.

The European foreigners on America's soil consciousness resolve is to use America for the establishment of a New Rome in the Western Hemisphere, as an artificial world created and controlled by foreigners of European homogenous men.

A Manifest Destiny to erase the females of America bloodlines from their Garden of Eden with

Earth and control all of their bloodlines to Earth in the Western Hemisphere.

If successful:

Mankind, now can extend the life of their artificial patriarchal culture system indefinitely, expand the development of man made products and inventions of artificial energy systems: pillaging by using the natural life resources within the eco-life support- system of America as its fuel and

The women of mankind using the males of America following patriarchy, as the host to keep their ability to live on America alive... They can extract the genetics in the blood from the males of America's connection to the soil of America

As in Rome, the economy of trade will be based on creating man made riches from the exploitation and consumption of the wealth in natural resources created as a part of the ecosystem life support for America- belonging to the Anisazi race of Peoples' blood line inheritance connection to America from Earth. The European foreigners started Laying claims over life essence with America as their (OUR) collective property; including the Anisazi females' life, children, and the genetics contained in her blood; Implementation of this process ensures successful dominance and expansion of mankind's race population into America and over other life essences for the planet Earth's created human races with environmental life support systems from the life nature of Earth. (Represented by people who look like the soil of the Earth.)

In order for the Destiny ideal of the race of foreigners to manifest:

1. The foreign European collective had to develop a system to stop Anisazi females to America from using her advanced technological power from Earth to continue supporting and sustaining the environmental life in America for Earth, and stop the transfer of the advanced technological knowledge based- skills for how to support their environmental life support system to the future generations born from Anisazi females.

2. Destroy the Anisazi culture: control/ direct everything created by the future generations of Anisazi people towards European foreigners use to manifest their new destiny.

3. European foreigners as people needed to remove the Anisazi population ability to use their tremendous wealth in natural resources developed over millions of years living in the Americas.

In order for the European foreigners to control the Anisazi females of Americas' production and fertility to reproduce their environmental life support system with the power in the essence of their bloodlines from America their home with Earth, and use all the developed natural wealth belonging to the Anisazi females of America's race of peoples. The invading European population must weaken thru de-population the Anisazi people born from Anisazi females of America from their home with Earth called America.

This effect can only be achieved by blocking the Anisazi females of America's collective ability to procreate, and support the life viability of the environment and soil to the future generations for the Anisazi females of America in America, and by changing the Anisazi males' allegiance to provide protection and structural support for the life of his bloodlines of people with the Earth inheritance he shares thru the essence from the blood of their MOTHERs to America.

"I have traveled across the length and breadth of America, and I have not seen one person who is a beggar, who is a thief, such wealth I have seen in this country, such high moral values, people of such caliber, I do not think we would ever conquer this country, unless we break the very backbone of this

*nation, which is **her spiritual (consciousness) and cultural heritage**, and therefore I propose we replace **HER** old and ancient education system, **her** culture, for if these people think that all that is foreign is good and greater than their own, they will lose their self-esteem, their native culture, and they will become what we want them to be, A TRULY DOMINATED NATION.."(comment written 1800's)*

The Anisazi people will have to be tricked into **not** fighting to save the lives of the females of America bloodline from their MOTHERS who continue to create the Anisazi females of Americas people, and carry in their blood the unconditional inheritance to the Earth soil named America, as their race home with Earth given to them by the planet Earth to be fruitful and multiply, and accept their race extermination by all means passively possible (political) to weaken them into voluntarily abandoning their ecosystem life support from their home with Earth to move to an artificial place as (immigrants) somewhere else on their planet Earth.

To accomplish this mission for getting rid of the population of Anisazi females of America and her huge population of people in the Americas. The European foreigners will have to:

1. Change the Anisazi Peoples' perception of reality of purpose with their life , especially the females.
2. Change the consciousnes way of thinking for the Anisazi males and females about themselves to their planet Earth and each other.
3. Remove/ disconnect / stop the intellectual connection with their innate conscious connection to their Earth within the Anisazi people that is awakened/ received from **respecting** their ancestral female connection, and self-determination power from America being their home with Earth.
4. Entrap the Anisazi people thru coercion, to break their allegiance to the Life covenant with Earth life, to support Nature and each other.
5. Coerce Anisazi females of America and her people to abandon their Earth purpose and choose to use their life towards indulging in entertainment for their physical comfort and accept their death as a consequence for the misuse of their innate power from Earth.

6. Influence the Anisazi people to ignore their ancestral connection to Earth of America in their blood and encourage their future generations to forfeit their home with Earth; by voluntarily keeping them ignorant about America their home with Earth; while they are influenced to move from their home with Earth to an artificial place on land....
7. Influence Anisazi males to stop supporting the continuation of their soul life bloodline within them, instead procreate with European foreign women; as a result, transfers the Anisazi females of Americas' genetic codes they inherited from their mother's bloodline inheritance from Earth, over the power of nature's life force with America.

To accomplish their ends, the European foreigners quickly resorted to a time tested mental technology developed by the Romans to cultivate the extermination of the indigenous Carthaginian / Nubian race of people, renamed Egyptians. Nubia at one time was a forest full of life, called the Fertile Crescent of the East. The Fertile Crescent of the East life blood(water) in the soil was consumed by the Romans (thru the use of Roman aqueduct system)and once depleted; turned the once water rich LIFE support system to maintain the abundance of plant systems ; creating the fertile crescent into a Lifeless or dead piece of Earth. A dessert.

The Roman destruction of this section with Earth, the home soil (Nubia) for the indigenous Carthaginian/Nubian people resulted in their extinction. Any area of Earth soil sited to be conquested by foreigners to be used for Roman European/ colonialism systematic consumption and eventual extermination is labeled by Roman/European foreigners as **"Africa"**.

Since the successful extermination of the indigenous Earth population race as Nubian/ Negro people with the Earth mass section located in the Middle section of the Eastern Hemisphere. The mental technology developed by the Romans have continued in its development and is used by Roman descendants as Europeans to passively take control over the different indigenous races of people's inhabiting different areas of Earth; and has spread over the last 5000 years into the mass colonization of complete continents of Earth; known as Africa, Asia, Australia, Central America, South America and India to name a few.

Colorism and Destruction

Can be conceived as far broader. As concerned with the colonization of knowledge- or categories as with its more well known modalities. The destructive, indeed genocidal consequences of Eurocentric concepts of social development..

> A. Dirk Moses- Department of History, University of Sidney

To start to accomplish this long- term goal, Roman/European foreigners set out to create an artificial kind of society and culture, based on the pillaging of all aspects of the Earth Life force nature living in a section to the planet Earth called Patriarchy. Patriarchy is an intellectual form of Warfare that is used against the natural innate Life consciousness of Earth living within Life's feminine emotional expression process that exists in all Earth created life forms.

This collective emotional expression of life process creates a heterogeneous society and heterosexual culture. . Patriarchy is the opposite a completely Homogeneous society and homosexual culture Patriarchy social culture aka male supremacy is used against the balance in heterogeneous societies and heterosexual cultures.

Patriarchy is a form of society based on reversing the egalitarian balance between the female and males in planetary societies and culture of Earth. Replacing it with an artificial social cast system that breeds hate elitism and oppression of peoples by using *artificial identities.*

In the Patriarchal society, the Roman/ European foreign collective dominates (including other men) in the society thru a cast system of Artificial identities. He /they have the power to accept or reject a persons planetary Earth LIFE right based on the category a person is profiled in. Rewards and penalties are metered out as a result from occupancy in one of these artificial categories. Prejudices are applied to the categories in which one is placed.

In the beginning, the ideal promoted by Roman/European foreigners to Anisazi males for the creation of a new society in America, the new society only included Roman /European men, women, children, and Anisazi males, as Americans. Anisazi females of America and their children were excluded. They represented the "other" or collateral (security of Deed), their lives are expendable and can be destroyed with impunity by those included in this new society. The Anisazi females and the children born from them, in the new American Patriarchal society were used for their Earth inheritance in economic commerce, as real estate collateral or chattel slaves for trade. Capturing the free females of America for their Earth inheritance to soil giving ownership as land in America, started the human trafficking of capturing the Anisazi female population living in the Americas.

Once in captivity, the once free Anisazi females of America on their soil are used for land title, along with industry ,personal comfort, and sexual recreation. This was a powerful lure to young Anisazi males for joining the new society to capture their young female kinfolk. The Roman/European foreigners who landed in North America and other parts of the Americas, quickly established a colony / base to start the Patriarchy trade in human trafficking for acquiring ownership over the females of America Earth inheritance to soil..

Now, in order to establish the conquest of the Anisazi race of people, using the new social vices against the Anisazi culture, the Roman/European foreigners needed the Anisazi males to adopt the warfare vice to use against their females, of Patriarchy as their new social culture.

 As a whole, the Anisazi race consisted of millions of males and 3 times as many millions of Anisazi females of America and children. It is well documented the indigenous population of America inhabited every inch in the Americas. Roman/European foreigners as Americans categorized the division of millions of indigenous people belonging to the indigenous race by being born from indigenous females' collective bloodline: as Nations, and sub-units of families/community as tribes. The Roman/European foreigners as Americans also divided the Anisazi peoples into separate categories based on their gender (Males and Females).

Picture above-Anisazi couple summer New York area 1670 (APHT Research Dept)

The whole race population of Anisazi females of America's people are now unknowingly being divided into two separate categories in the new emerging Patriarchal society.

Using this kind of environ- <u>mental</u> technology vice upon the Anisazi Peoples of Americas; the Roman/Europeans foreigners as Americans, established new artificial categories for the people of America, using labels that represent different process sequences of the ethnic cleansing system, as names to use for ethnic/ heritage identity by the foreigners.

The new ethnic cleansing labels as identity will keep the population for Anisazi females of America invisible in their artificial Roman/European patriarchal world, making it easier for maintaining the long- term process towards the extermination of the Anasazi females of America race bloodlines of peoples from their Earth soil life support as a part of America.

Once captured in America and placed in the new Patriarchal social system, the Anisazi females of America, male and female descendants, are given new classification identity as Negro and kept their ancestral original Earth connection to America identity for indigenous (Indian) children as mullatto. Children born from the children of captive Anisazi females of America were considered descendants of Indians of America for 3 generations or 39 years.

The races in the new Patriarchal society are to be White (European), Black / Negro (Anasazi females and children living in captivity with Earth inheritance), and Red (Anisazi males born free before the establishment of patriarchy-(first Americans of the United States) under European terms.

The ideals for this new form of society became the lure Europeans used to divide the Anisazi males from their life lines with their Anisazi females. The Roman/European foreigners promoted their society based on artificial ideals that glorified males who chose to live homogenous under patriarchy as men, and made promises for male only individual self-determination instead of collective preservation to the young Anisazi males for changing their allegiance from protecting their bloodline inheritance to their people and Earth soil ;to the establishing, building as Americans of a new nation state for a patriarchal society and culture.

Unknowingly to the Anisazi Males, the promises made of ideals of equal inclusion and shared power in the governing of the new patriarchal society governed by Roman/ European foreigners using their Earth soil America; for their support: are promises the Roman/ European foreigners will never honor – (ideals that will never work for the benefit of the Anisazi people as a whole, only to Anasazi males individually and never bring justice collectively to the Anisazi male collective).

The Ideals Europeans promised to Anisazi males (if they betrayed their Conscious Nature): they could live in a world that is a utopia for Anisazi Males, "the American Dream"; living their lives for personal comfort , they could experience their wildest cardinal dreams, exploiting the Anisazi females life force for physical SEX instead of emotional intimacy, and avoid direct accountability consequences from breaking their allegiance to their purpose given to them from Earth as a part of the nature with their species: as support and protectors of the home with Earth for the Anisazi people created by the Anisazi females of America.

However, there was an exchange for this ideal American Dream. The new cultural society for Men will be governed by European foreigners and their Laws The Anisazi males could join this new society if they were willing to participate in the captivity of their mothers, sisters, for the use of their inheritance to Earth soil shared with the males as belonging to the collective blood of Anisazi females of America, and rob/ pillage their people of their the tremendous wealth and knowledge from their heritage culture to build a new nation using their soil

. Every Anisazi female of America has an individual Earth inheritance to the soil of America They are indigenous to America and in possession of existing rights to the soil

For the purpose of acquiring the soil of America to use as land for the new Nation.. The Roman/European foreigners placed a very high value of exchanged for their material inventions with the Anasazi males wanting to trade with the American men. The Roman/ European foreigners as Americans only acceptable trade exchange for material trinkets and beads or other inventions with Anisazi men is the bodies of free Anisazi females of America alive or dead. If dead(represented by their scalps) or their children, each is worth 400 acres of America's soil.

Now, listen to me carefully child...Under this new form of social culture being established called Patriarchy; under the original ethnic identity classification by European foreigners as Americans, for the whole Anisazi human race of America is Amerindians ,the Anisazi male born free remained FREE, classified under the original European identity of Indian race sub term as RED Savage.

However, the term Indian did not apply to Anisazi females and children still living free in America. The Roman/ European men as Americans started in 1705 a NEW classification category for all Anisazi females of America as "Negro " meaning the indigenous race of people with the blood of America inheritance to soil, to be captured for conquest under "Freedom". In other words, people to be captured and used as money or real estate property, people being denied their existing Earth rights - the right to live with self-determination as free with their Earth right inheritance and possessions; therefore people to be "enslaved "with a new term for their portion of the Anisazi female race population of America as "black"; thus being regarded as the "OTHER" a separate nation from the Americans "United States" living in their home to Earth inheritance within the Americas.

Under the new artificial Patriarchal social category for the race population of Anisazi females of Americas identity of Negro, the indigenous brown-skinned curly-haired Anisazi females and children born in captivity, are stripped of their fundamental Earth rights to their Earth bloodline inheritance to America and are stigmatized for the process of being dehumanized to seeing themselves as being a piece of real estate property or land deed.

Now, as Negroes the new generations of America will not be respected for their unconditional right from Earth as having a right to remain free to develop on their inheritance soil. In this new form of society Anisazi females and children will be hunted, and killed or captured, to be sold/ bought for their inheritance to the Earth soil, called America. To be Used as American currency for trade as slaves for the rest of their lives, AND the INHERITANCE belonging to them TO EARTH FROM THEIR HOME with EARTH America, will be considered as confiscated property (land) for private use forever in the Americas by ALL American MEN.

Picture above: Captured FREE Anasazi females and children in America to be traded as Negros and used as "Slaves "for the establishment of Patriarchy in Freedom. (AHPT Research dept.)

For over 150 years Anisazi females of America and their children, were massacred in their villages for their scalps or kidnapped for captivity to be converted into slaves and exchanged as real estate property. Millions of Anisazi females of America were being exported to the West Indies to be sold for their horticultural(planting) technology as planters in commerce. Now in captivity they had to learn how to survive living "in Freedom. Freedom will be the new way of life for the remaining future generations of Anisazi people living in America, their home with Earth.

Over time Anisazi males hunting for FREE indigenous (Anisazi) females and children in America to trade as real estate for whiskey and weapons, expanded all over the Americas. The Anisazi males who were willing to betray their Earth covenant and change their allegiance to the invading Europeans foreigners as Americans adopted their genocidal ways of social development, and used the artificial European terms to identify themselves. Meanwhile, Anisazi females and their children's lives and culture, in America their home with Earth is being destroyed. Anisazi females of America are being forced to accept an artificial way of living their purpose to Earth with new dehumanizing collective terms of identity for themselves as niggas, blacks, coons, . These names are still used today to identify them as their public ethnic and social identity in the new Patriarchal society established on their life blood soil " America" .

As a result of the constant kidnapping massacres, dehumanizing treatment, sexual torture, and physical violence against them from the invading Americans establishing the United States patriarchal society. A society that only recognized the race of peoples born indigenous to America from the female bloodlines with America, as people to be exterminated from life in America by the United States implementation of the process for genocide of their people in the American society at large from their home with Earth.

MeMa, what happened to the elders of the Anisazi people and the people who did not want to sell their females and children as land?

For thousands of years, the Anisazi people respected their allegiance to their planet Earth, section to Earth as America, and lived by the principles governing Life of Earth as the foundation for their culture consciousness, along with all Earth created people living freely on their Earth inheritance section.. The elders understood the vital purpose to the planet Earth given to females as the creators of human Life consciousness, and the power inherited from Earth that all females possess to her soil.. They were protected because they knew how to use the power of nature within them from their home with Earth soil. The elders were able to combat the European influence on young Anisazi males to betray their natural Male conscious to protect their bloodlines from females, instead of falling for the mental tricks taught by European foreigner's that homo sexualized them thru (misogyny), disconnecting them from their inner power as Males and enslaving the males to become homogenous as MEN.

The war being waged against Earth life consciousness from the intellectual influence to misuse Nature leading to hedonism and death kept the Anisazi people constantly at war with each other and living without trust, security and peace.

However, Influencing the young Anisazi males to abandon their covenant with Earth to live in Patriarchy was not the extent of the arsenal of weapons used for race extermination by the invading Roman/European foreigners brought with them from Europe. Biological warfare or diseases. Diseases were imported by the invading people to use against the populations in the Americas. Small pox, Malaria, Syphilis, Gonorrhea, Measles, Influenza , Cholera just to name a few. The biological weapons of warfare as diseases effected the oldest of the Elders (100 years – 150 years old). As the elders started to die off at younger ages a lot of the wisdom from their knowledge died with them, meanwhile the younger generations of females were being killed or captured. The people who survived from attack by Diseases .Their blood developed immunity to many of the foreign diseases plaguing them and quickly replenished their indigenous Anisazi/Negro populations in those areas in the Americas.

As time moved forward the effects of the weapons created to breakdown the Anasazi male and female natural consciousness of unity between them took a toll- without a defense to stop the addictions to whiskey, rape, and killing females for scalps was steady taking over Anisazi young males natural consciousness, it caused them to spread the pillaging of villages for the young innocent and beautiful Anisazi females and children, to trade as land with European men for whiskey and weapons, grew like wild fire.

Every place in America Roman/European foreigners traveled, wars broke out between Anisazi communities as a result of the crimes committed against the members in the families. The crimes angered the Anisazi males to abandon their cultural heritage systems (love for life) and wage war (revenge) by making allegiances with their enemies to cause harm or death against the offending kinfolk,by attacking the offending kinfolk females, who by nature are not at war with them, therefore became defenseless against them.

Anisazi males had to constantly fight with each other to their death or enslavement over stopping the trade for enslavement of the female members in their families or rectifying the crimes of rape and scalping being committed against the Anisazi family members they loved; Example: A cousin came to make a visit while the males are out hunting, kidnaps the young girls and children, kills and scalps their mothers, then burns down the village to cover their tracks , the cousins uses the scalps of the females and children to exchange for a metal pocket knife and some whiskey.

As the influence from the ideology of patriarchy and the addiction to whiskey worsened. The unconscious's Anisazi Male as men continued to fight with each other over the Anisazi females of their race to use for European trade. Millions of Anisazi females and their children were being captured to be converted into slaves or being killed for their scalps by young Anisazi males addicted to whiskey and following the influence of Patriarchy by European foreigners as Americans and their own men.

Anisazi males collectively invested in the American Dream, of becoming Men. Ignored some Principled facts for the principles of life operating as nature with Earth, and what happens when they abandon their purpose for life of the whole.

You see child, The European secret promises made to Anisazi males if they support the genocidal establishment of Patriarchy, was they will be able to use mental vices against and physical trauma on the consciousness of their female captives to control a females life building energy to use for male comfort and desires. The trick in this promise to young Anisazi males for an artificial ideal is, the ideal goes against the LAWS OF their own NATURE-

Now Child ...the laws of nature don't change for anything or anybody.......

Forcing the Anisazi females into emotional trauma and repression to support an artificial purpose for their life, instead of supporting the Earth fertility, and building the life environment of Earth, causes the male who exploits and capitalizes on their emotional violations, to loses the capacity to develop into his highest Potential of power from Life of Earth as the counterpart of the whole natural unit as a Male/ Female as (1) or actualize his highest purpose inherited to him by the Earth. …. Instead, he becomes weak and full of FEAR, he remains in the state of a child, to follow as a man child or true man, he lacks the strength to lead as an adult Male.. The Anisazi male who at one time was the most dominant force and intellectual power for the Earth, remains in the mental state of a boy(self-centered), to remain as adult -child instead of Males over men. The consequence from the nature of life removes the Anisazi males (now as American Indians) ability for pro-activity to collectively defend themselves...

In other words the once powerful Anisazi male's protectors of America lose his ability to be pro-active against defending the aggressions against him individually or collectively by the collective of European men. The consequences to the Anisazi male is he becomes as powerless as his female/ mothers and soil he enslaved.

 In the laws of nature, as long as you are supporting your individual- collective purpose for Earth life within nature, your life is supported and empowered by highest force on Earth as nature, when you do not support your purpose for life within nature you are left with only your physical power to use, and can quickly be destroyed by the Karma of nature. Anisazi males can never remain Free; while there Anisazi female mothers are "in Freedom". The American Dream of Patriarchy is a one way ticket to the Twilight ZONE.

In other words it is a mental trick used to get the Anisazi males to curse themselves and lose their own power with Life and destroy their heritage bloodline and culture that's supports their power, allowing European foreigners and others to build on their home soil with Earth.

Another ignored secret behind the European ideal, promoted as the American Dream to Anisazi (American Indian) men, comes from basic facts about Nature; Females produce Males, Males do not reproduce themselves. Anisazi males as American Indian men are born FREE to the Earth from FREE Anisazi females who carry the human genetics from their home of Earth soil. When the young Anisazi females were forced into the new foreign controlled cultural systems for genocide, all the Anisazi females of America race are considered as slaves to be used by men along with their soil inheritance (real estate) and personal property; as American Negro women. The new generations of Anisazi males born from Anasazi females are no longer considered FREE as their American Indian grandfathers, they are not considered a part of the original Americans, they are considered captive slaves as Negro's living "in FREEDOM" as descendants from Mothers who are captives from America for their Earth inheritance soil to America.

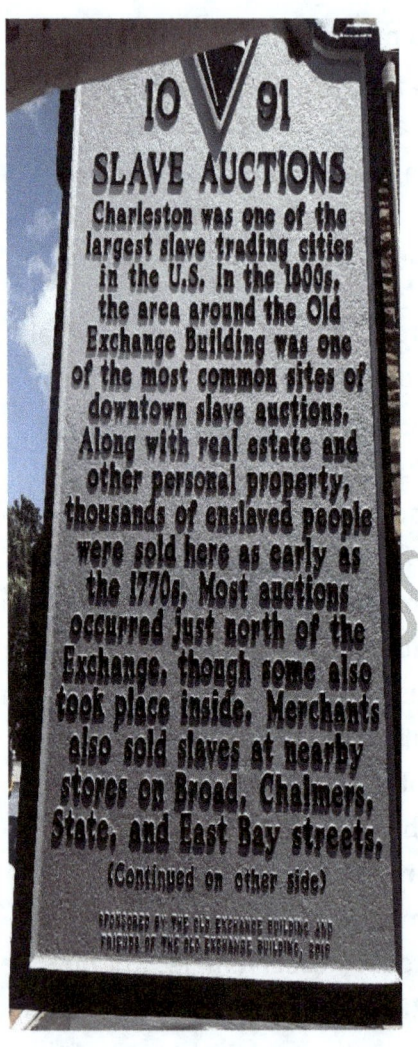

  Read carefully, "thousands of enslaved people were sold here as early as the 1770's. "look at the dates, the establishment of slavery in Charleston started as early as 1770. Not before…

Below:

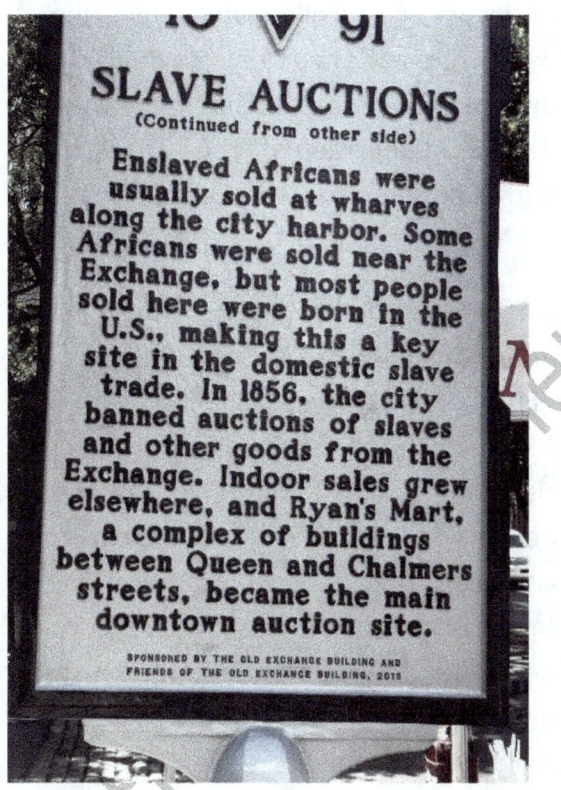

Read carefully: *"but most people sold "Here" were born in the US.* Meaning the majority of people traded and sold as slaves in Charleston ,SC.were born from Anisazi females of America. They were not imported people from Africa. They are captured Anisazi females of America being sold as real estate and personal property. Also note *" In 1856, the city banned auctions of slaves and other goods from the exchanged."* Slavery Started in Charleston , Sout Carolina 1770 ended in 1856 "Banned autions of people of America as real estate and their personal property.

Once the original Anisazi men born FREE *before* the accepted enslavement and alledged confiscation of all Anisazi women inheritance to soil of America died out, there were no more Anisazi males under the first artificial classification of Free as American Indians left in their home soil with Earth as America..

As a result of the elimination of FREE Anisazi males as American Indians {who are the original men along with European men who helped in creating the United States}. The future generations of Anisazi males born from Anisazi females **lost their ability to be considered as free** under the category of American Indian. They also lost their position with the United States to hold the United States accountable for the promises made to the Anisazi men as American Indians. They lost the collective recognized right to have equal self - determination as being a part of the New Patriarchal society as Americans their grandfathers helped to establish by practicing genocidal warfare against the Anisazi/ American Indian/ Negro females of America in their shared home by blood of those females to a home with Earth soil, called America.

Now that the new generations of Anisazi males are ***trapped in the Karma of their forefathers***.

A new level of genocide could be implemented against the people of America.

European foreign women as Americans can practice miscegenation against the blood to the Anisazi females of America. The children born by European foreign women with Anisazi males can now claim the Anisazi male's position as FREE or American Indians of the United States as an people.

Picture above; Anisazi male with European girl as - the new Cherokee American Indian 1932 NC (AHPT Research dept)

The new group of hybrid people as Native Americans to the United States developed from children born from European females who procreated with Anisazi males regardless of classification as American Indian or Negro.

As though females of America descendants are not Americans. The European woman placed her genetically mixed children (half breeds) into the artificial category for the Americans as descendants to indigenous men of America called "Native Americans", adopting indigenous names created by indigenous America men supporting patriarchy , completely blocking the indigenous Anisazi females to America people from being respected for their rightful heritage identity claim as the indigenous Peoples of America from their mothers and fathers.

The elimination of the FREE Anisazi males as American Indians opened the door for the United States to eliminate the future generations for the Anisazi race of people collectively from their American his-story as being recognized and respected for their truth as the direct continuation for the original Anisazi females of America, their cultural contributions from their heritage culture in their home with Earth called America.

Apache boy with face and legs painted. Apache Indian boy put on display for whites... 1929 . (AHPT Research dept)

Soon after the Patriarchal process began the United States was formed to institutionalize Patriarchy as the newly established governing society and the development of a social culture for the perpetual enslavement for extermination of the Anisazi females and children of America to continue. The government established as the United States will maintain the control over the home with Earth soil belonging to the Anisazi race as Negro peoples for the benefit of the

Roman/European foreign implant as Americans on America as their new home land. .

So Me Ma!!!, What happened to the Anisazi people after there was no more free Anisazi males left?

Now, the time has come to implement the next phase of the trick on the Anisazi race of people. It is time to remove their mental connection from the new generations of people to the Anisazi females' population with America from their natural home with Earth called America.

" *Thomas Jefferson as President of the United States changed the term RED used to represent the race color for the /dark skin Earth people who look liked the soil of America or Anisazi Peoples to represent the color of death or DEAD BLOOD, so the brown-crayon sketch is rubbed out, and the canvas is ready for a picture of manhood more like God's own image.*"

"Oliver Wendell Holmes rejoiced in the elimination of Indians on aesthetic grounds."
The dark-skinned Anisazi race of people as American Indians and Negros would no longer be recognized under the original term for the dark-skinned people who looked like the soil, as Red. Now the race of people whose home with Earth soil as America is now artificially vanished.

In the 1900's the new term for the dark-skinned Anisazi race of people is changed again- from brown= red, now brown= black . As a result of changing the ethnic and racial identity terms used by American people for the Anisazi people, the Anisazi race of dark- skinned or brown people and their civilization would vanish under European American classifications from their home to Earth soil, termed America.

The section of Earth called America could now be completely severed from the connection to the Anisazi female race of America peoples as Negro, and used to solidify the conquest over America to use as the United States new homeland for the Roman/ European foreigners as American people; to complete the manifestation of their ideal destiny..

During the late 1800's in the period call reconstruction, the Europeans claiming the Americas as their new Earth home taught thru free public education to the Anisazi children of America as Negros: the Negro race of peoples are descendants of Slaves(Anisazi females of America) are inferior people that should not continue to be fruitful and multiply in their home with Earth America, and there is no home with Earth for them, they belonged to the dead or no longer living people from the desert of Africa in Egypt.

Instead of the TRUTH about their unconditional home to EARTH SOIL being America, which the United States is destroying by stripping the natural environment of America for use as an new homeland suitable only for their race to live on.

So MeMa, what happened from the tricks used on the original/ indigenous race of Anisazi females of America PEOPLE's new generations living in their home with Earth in America, called the American Indians?

Well child, the campaign for our complete extermination as genocide still plagues us. Our people still have not realized the ideals promoted as blessings with living under Freedom given to us from the Europeans has been our curse. The American dream has taken us from being a FREE, strong, wealthy and powerful people with the Earth to an intellectually ignorant, poor in consciousness, physically weak people, who have an allegiance to all forms of artificial vices used to exploit and rob life from them, leaving them on the brink of extinction as a people living in FREEDOM.

In conclusion

Yeah, we are still here. At one time we inhabited all of America, now we barely inhabit 1/8 of our home to Earth , and have control over even less….

Today we struggle to live as ***educated or assimilated/ cultivated*** slaves in the hostile, artificial world created by Europeans foreigners as Americans, while hiding from our truth " We are America" believing in the political propaganda ideal of racial equality, with the illusions we are **Artificial** Americans, in a country where the National policy is to keep systematically exterminating them.

Today, the Anisazi female of America race of people no longer have a respect for the nature that created them, nor for their home with Earth America. They no longer uphold life, they consume their beautiful life force power in all forms of hedonisms and narcissisms. They worship death, to their special gift from Earth to life with Earth.

The lost children of America break most of the natural laws that will protect them from the exploitation of death. The Anisazi females of America are not fruitful nor do they want to ensure the continuation of life and the ancestral bloodiness in our home to Earth by keeping their precious bloodline alive.

The lost children of America are trapped in a never ending war of influences of all forms of homosexuality and hedonism, that is being used against them to break the principles of Earth nature power in their blood ,from the bloodlines in their mothers, that can change the horrible consequences awaiting for them from the mistakes of the generations before them..

Today the lost children of America are the unconscious, they are the ones who act like savages.

A few hundred years ago we were once a Principled people called the Anisazi people of America. As a result of indulging in the foreign influences of social development from others, unfortunately our forefathers following their lead , labeled as American Indians, changed to the Negro Americans, are again giving the people of America another new identity name to mark our position in our extinction from our soil, America.

The new name given for our people to adopt is "African Americans", meaning people who are unwanted refugees from America in America .Our dark skin color that was once named red , changed to brown, is now changed to the color of death as "black". Today our children do not know why there is so much hate and racism against them Now, our children believe that the life given to them from the precious blood of America from their mothers is worthless and they belong somewhere in the dessert of Africa. They do not realize they hold the key to the ultimate power of the planet Earth in their blood to America. It is this precious essence they carry is why they can stop the death of our bloodlines. The power of America is with them, HoHo

The story you have just read is a brief overview of the omitted heritage story of America and how the Females of America peoples as Amerindians became Negros ,blacks and now African Americans. Knowledge about the past can give the insight needed to understand the condition we see happening to our people today, and give the clarity to the lost generations of the children of America of why the Karma of the past is plaguing them into self- destruction. It is time to stop being a victim to the tricks of illusion of man, and return to the way of consciousness of our Anisazi ancestors' blood that lives within us. We must return back to life back to reality, to stop our life destruction.

To learn more about our Amerindian culture and home to Earth as America,   learn how to live by our ancestral principles and become a part of the Anisazi Heritage people's. If you are a descendant of Negro ancestry. You are not an immigrant in America. Save your Earth rights to your human rights to live in America.

Register with the America Heritage Registry @ www.fiaah.org

 Help support our right to live with our planet Earth now and in the future, support the

 "**We are America** "petition. www.fiaah.org

Quantum Leap SLC Publications published the first books in the United States on the heritage of black "America" . Publications published by Quantum Leap S.L.C. are the following:

The black American Handbook for the survival thru the 21st Century vol 1   The forgotten truth behind racism in America ,
Author RaDine Amen-ra

The black American Paradigm: American Heritage History in America- Human Rights vs Civil Rights
Author RaDine America

The Hidden Ancestral Identity of the Negro. The truth Euro- America DARE not tell.
Author RaDine America

Getting out the System. Free vs Freedom What's the Difference?
Author RaDine America

A short story of the "Anisazi Peoples"

Author RaDine America. Harrison

It is time to learn the truth about what is happening to our life, before it is too late!

To contact the Foundation for Indigenous America of Anisazi Heritage (F.I.A.A.H) call 1-877-571-0788 or 304-212-2362   or email us at admin@fiaah.org www,fiaah.org

It is time to Recognize, Realize and Respect who we are.

A People who do not know the truth about their past-are destined to perish from it.

RaDine America Harrison

www.ingramcontent.com/pod-product-compliance
Lightning Source LLC
Chambersburg PA
CBHW050607300426
44112CB00013B/2117